A GREEN WITCH'S POCKET BOOK OF WISDOM

Big Little Life Tips

Robin Rose Bennett
Illustrations by Gail Stoughton

A Green Witch's Pocket Book of Wisdom—Big Little Life Tips
Copyright © 2023 by Robin Rose Bennett

All rights reserved. No part of this book may be used or reproduced in any manner whatsoever including Internet usage, without written permission of the author.

Cover Design by Nicla DiCosmo
Illustrations by Gail Stoughton
Book design by Maureen Cutajar

ISBN: 978-0-9821082-5-3

"Magical, comforting, wise. Working with *A Green Witch's Pocket Book of Wisdom* feels like knocking on the door of an enchanted cottage at the edge of the woods. Inside is the elder witch of your dreams, ready to give you the answer you seek. Inside is everything you need to create a life of magic and wellbeing."

—Asia Suler, author of Mirrors in the Earth

"Wisdoms are insights that meaningfully illuminate the magic that is this life and the world we inhabit, reminders to be awake and aware in the moments we occupy. Robin Rose Bennett, and her newest book, *A Green Witch's Pocket Book of Wisdom*—are full of such wisdom."

—jim mcdonald, herbalist

"This book is a supportive friend, ally, and teacher all wrapped into one beautiful book. Its musings, poems, and perspectives offer wisdom, new ways of thinking, and kind magic. The work and writing of Robin Rose Bennett are foundational for anyone on the Green Witch's path, but this book is also for anyone navigating what it means to be human. Consider *A*

Green Witch's Pocket Book of Wisdom a lantern, a guide through the forest of life, a reminder that enchantment and awe are possible."

—Kate Belew, poet & green witch

"You are always on your path. This deceptively simple guidebook has prompt after prompt to remind you of that, and to ease your journey. Stock up; you're going to want to give a copy of *A Green Witch's Pocketbook of Wisdom* to most everyone you know."

—Kathy Biehl, professional astrologer, podcaster, and contributor to *Your Guide to Self-Discovery* (Llewellyn Worldwide)

"So grateful for this treasure trove of insightful gems! *A Green Witch's Pocket Book of Wisdom* is gorgeously illustrated and Robin's favorite teachings and age-old wisdoms are conveyed in her unique voice. Another true offering of Love and Guidance from this very Wise Woman."

—Lata Chettri-Kennedy, green witch herbalist, proprietress of Flower Power Herbs and Roots, Inc.

*This book is dedicated in gratitude to my teachers,
And to you.*

Introductions

Robin Rose Bennett

I am an herbalist, an Earth-based green witch with a Buddhist bent, and I confess that in this current incarnation you can't take the Jewish mother out of the green witch.
Eat your vegetables. Go outside and play.
Be kind to one another. I care about you.

Gail Stoughton

I am a fine artist and teacher and enjoy working in a variety of mediums. I'm also an organic gardener, and an active advocate for animals, social justice, and the natural environment.
I celebrate that special part of me that remains untamed. In this garden of life, I will always be a wildflower.

A Note to the Reader

My personal favorite way to read *A Green Witch's Pocket Book of Wisdom—Big Little Life Tips* is to practice bibliomancy with it.

If you are unfamiliar with the term, *bibliomancy* is the practice of asking for guidance, then opening a book anywhere at "random" to see what message you have opened to.

For my friends, clients, students and family, the results have often felt uncanny.

You may, of course, read this book any way you like: forward, backward, cover-to-cover, or in bits and pieces. I am thrilled that you are at last able to hold it in your hands!

Blessed be

Love,
Robin Rose

~*~

Foreword

"To be awake costs no less than everything, but it's worth the price."

The above quote was written by my first spiritual teacher, June Graham Spencer, a wise woman with an extraordinary zest for living. She helped others to face their shadows, as she faced hers, in order to live life to the fullest. It is in this spirit that I offer my *Green Witch's Pocket Book of Wisdom*. June followed her own version of a Buddhist path, especially in the last decades of her life, but she often referred to herself as a red-headed witch. And so she was.

Trust Life

Cultivate trust in the goodness of life,
in its cycles of loss and gain.

When the inevitable challenges arise, you will
move through them with more love and grace.
Author Byron Katie counsels us to "Love What
Is." This is not only a ticket to freedom, it also
opens the door to receiving unending support for
transformation from the Universe.

Open to Magic

As you open yourself to seek
and discover the magic of life,
you'll find it is everywhere.
You'll become a magnet for helpful
synchronicity.
Magic will find you!

The "Real World" Is Found in Nature's Ongoing Cycles of Transformation

Get real! Wherever you live, attune to the underlying reality of Nature. Everything and everyone is coming to be and passing away, cycling through birth, growth, decay, death and rebirth. Become aware of the rhythms of the seasons, the rising and setting of the sun, the waxing and waning of the moon, the tides of the oceans.

Being in resonance with Nature strengthens your inner peace and stability.

Who Am I, and to What Am I Connected?

Emilie Conrad, founder of Continuum, introduced me to this fundamental inquiry.

I suggest you delve into it again and again. It will steer you toward self-awareness and toward cultivating your relationships with whatever is "true north" for you.

You Are Sacred

There is only one you. You matter. You count. You add to the whole. The world would not be the same without you in it.

What Makes Life Juicy For You?

What makes life fun, exciting, and meaningful?
Dare to find, and claim, whatever makes you
want to get out of bed in the morning, and greet
the new day with a smile in your heart.

You deserve that!

Whatever You Are Seeking Is Also Seeking You

When your desire springs from the truth of your being Spirit will conspire to bring you together with what you long for.

Practice Presence

Entering fully into any moment as it is will set you free.
Paradoxically, it takes time and practice to learn *how* to be here now.
Witness how entangled you feel when you wish the moment were different than it is.

And when you say,
"I'm getting there," try this instead:
"I'm getting here."

Ask Expansive Questions

The answers aren't as important as the questions.
Find the questions that guide you to live the kind
of life you wish to lead.

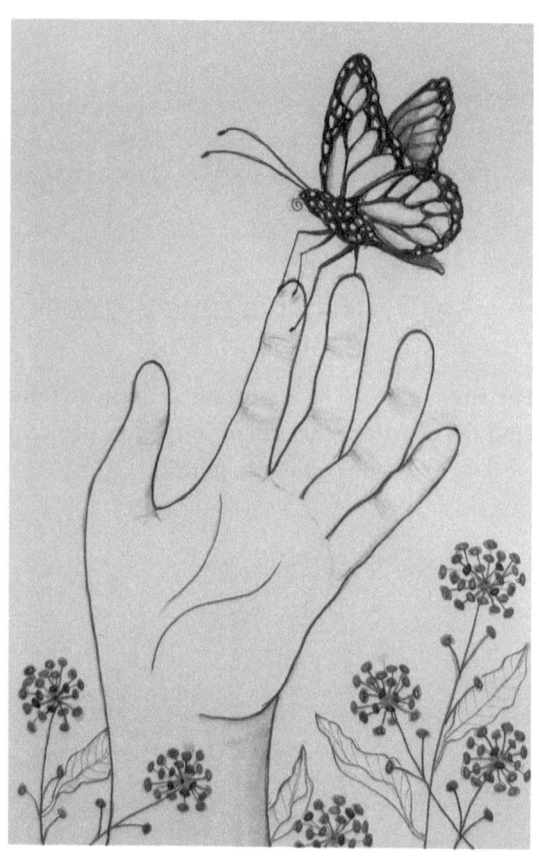

There Is Only Now and It Is Alive With Infinite Possibility

Open to the magic of this moment as it comes to be. Let it go as it passes away. Be present to the next moment that arises.

The past can only be the past when you let it go.

Put Love First

When you prioritize loving over being loved, being understood, or being right, the rewards reveal themselves in the experience.

It is simple, but not easy. Putting love first is a practice. When you choose to put love first, everything else falls into place.

The Most Difficult Passages in Our Lives Often Lead Us to Grace

We all resist experiences of illness, disappointment, failure, loss, and betrayal, yet they happen nonetheless. Exchange resistance for curiosity. Ask, "How can I make this my ally?" It helps open new doors.

Worry Is a Form of Unconscious Hexing

Thoughts are powerful. When you worry incessantly about someone, fretting about something that could go wrong as if it were bound to happen, you feed it energy.

When you notice yourself doing this, offer a blessing to counter it. For example, "I'm so worried that my son will die if he keeps using drugs," might be followed by "I see my son being held in safety. I see him coming through this challenge healthy, whole, and wiser than before." Your blessing may inspire and catalyze helpful ideas and actions, too.

Asking For Help—And Being Open to Receive It— Are Vital Life Skills That Are Crucial to Self-Care

Self-care doesn't mean you have to do everything by and for yourself. Whether you are asking Spirit, your neighbor, a family member, or a stranger, be willing to be humble, to be vulnerable. Give someone else the opportunity to experience the satisfaction that comes from being able to help another.

Allies Are Everywhere

You have allies everywhere, seen and unseen,
known and unknown. Call on them. And
sometimes *you* will be called, silently or out loud,
to be the ally someone else needs, an ally they
might not have realized they had
until you showed up.

"Alone" Is an Illusion

Believing in the illusion of separation is so painful. It is often said that we are born alone and die alone. As to our birth, our mothers would surely disagree. And as for death, we "return" to the oneness we never actually leave.

The truth is, we are all in this together.
The difference between Alone and All One is one
L: Love

Everything on Earth Speaks and Listens in Its Own Way

You have to slow down to listen to a tree.
You have to stop to hear the song in a stone.

Heed Your Dreams

Learn the uniquely personal, symbolic language of your dreams. The same symbols and metaphors will likely show up in your meditations, too. Listen to your inner guidance; it will help you create a more deeply satisfying life.

We Are Always Bringing Our Dreams
—And Our Nightmares—
Into Being

You are a powerful creator.
What nightmare is it time to banish?
What dream is it time to embrace?

Collectively, we are midwifing a new way of being in the world, a way of compassion and connection, of respect and justice. Together we contribute to everything that becomes manifest.

All Creation Begins in the Imagination

We are all dreaming this world into being, consciously and unconsciously.

Let's imagine the most beautiful possible present, and work together to make it so.

Relax into Becoming Your Authentic Self

Be yourself. Expressing who you really are inside will bring you greater contentment, and benefit those with whom you share yourself.

Make Space For Every Part of Yourself to Have a Safe Place to Be

A rose would never think, *I like my flowers, but my thorns are ugly*. Pushing part of yourself away never works. None of us is just one thing; we are multi-faceted.

Every part of you has or had a purpose. If it's time to let some aspect go, compassionate self-acceptance will help the parts you've outgrown to fall away naturally.

Lighten Up

Sometimes it's good to take yourself more lightly, less seriously. Balance heaviness by letting more light/ness in.

Don't *Should* on Yourself

Try substituting the word *could* for *should* in sentences such as: "I should return that call ... do the dishes ... apologize."

Should takes away autonomy and robs you of energy. *Could* acknowledges freedom of choice and gives you energy.

My teacher June used to say, "Don't *should* on me and I won't *should* on you."

It Is Enough Just to Be

When you feel pushed and pulled by the pressure to get things done, or if you're plagued by thoughts that who and what you are is not enough, repeat this invocation aloud. Say it slowly three times. Let it land in your body. Feel the truth of it.

It can help you feel more relaxed and at peace, which, incidentally, will yield better results in whatever you are doing.

Instead Of Saying: "I Have To ____," Explore Saying: "I Get To ____."

You *get* to do the laundry because you have clothes to wear and water to wash them with. You *get* to do the dishes because you had food to eat. Lucky you!

Reframing your perspective and restating it **aloud** presses a re-set button in your neural pathways.

The former drags your energy down, while the latter uplifts and brings more light, spaciousness and gratitude into your life.

Thanks to astrologer Caroline Casey for introducing me to this practice.

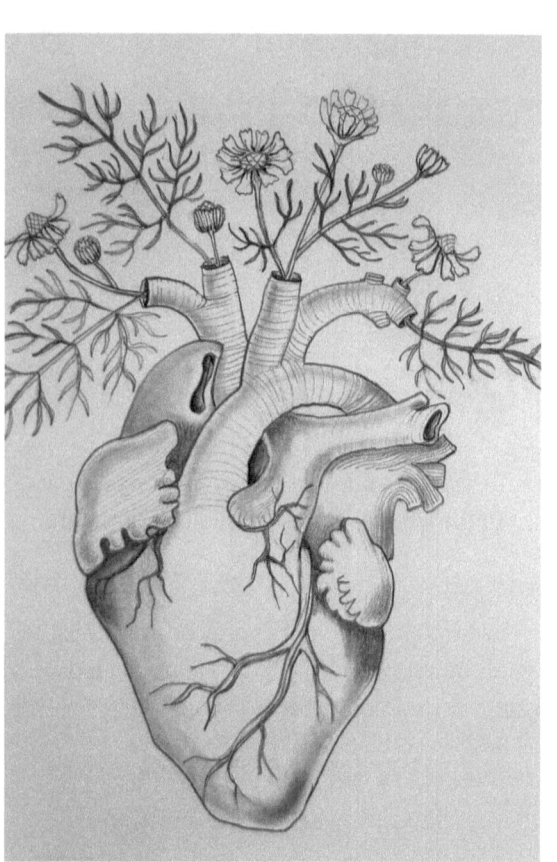

Allow Your Heart to Open

Let the armor around your heart soften. No doubt you put it there to protect yourself, but now it's time to let it melt away so your heart can love freely. Having an open heart doesn't mean you are a pushover or have to be "nice" all the time.

You can say NO with an open heart.

Learn to Say *No*

You are allowed to say *No*.
It is a complete sentence.

You can explain "why not" if you *choose* to,
but you don't ever *have* to.

What You Do to Another, You Do to Yourself
What You Do For Another, You Do For Yourself

Everything in this life is a mirror,
reflecting you back to yourself.

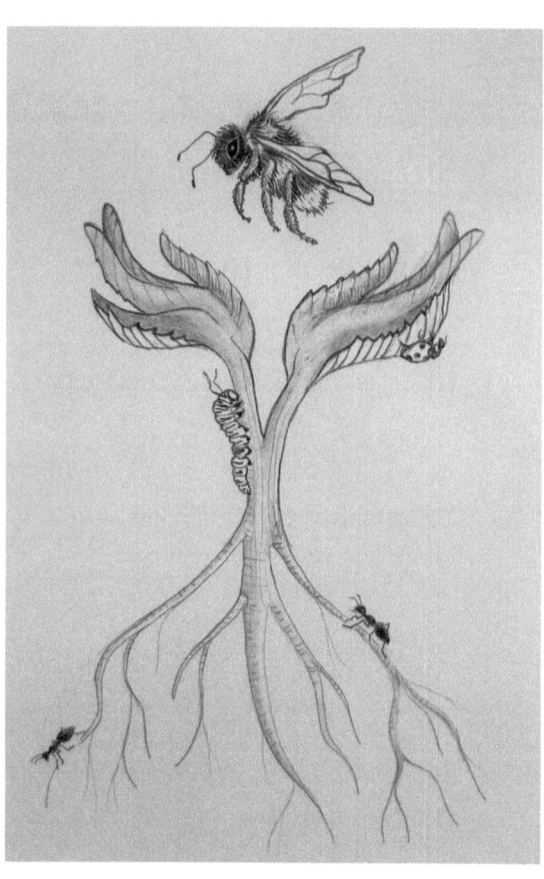

Plants Are Generous Beings

Plants provide the very air we breathe; they give us life. They also freely give us beauty, food, medicine, clothing, and shelter. Please sit with a plant today and offer your thanks.

I am grateful to herbalist Susun Weed for guiding me to live in conscious relationship with the green beings.

Plants Know Who They Are

I've never met a daisy who wished she smelled like lavender, nor an oak tree who felt inferior for not being as flexible as willow.

When you ingest, imbibe, inhale, or sit in meditation with any plant with respect and gratitude, that plant will help you center in the truth of your own being. Plants will help you know who you are, too.

Become Who You Came Here to Be, Yourself

This is why we are here.

You Are Love Incarnate

Mostly we cover up our love with heavy protective overcoats. Strip off the overcoats of needing to look cool or smart, needing to be liked or in control, and little by little you will bask in the love that you truly are. And so will everyone around you!

Find Your Tribe

Brene Brown said, "Don't seek to fit in. Seek to find where you belong." These are wise words to live by. To fit in, we try to change who we are. Belonging welcomes us *as* we are.

If the Story You're Telling Yourself is Causing You to Close Your Heart, Change It to One That Invites Your Heart to Open

"I'll never trust anyone again."
Could become:

"Trusting someone who betrayed me hurt like hell. Were there signs along the way I didn't want to see? I'll pay attention and listen to my intuition more carefully now.
I'm learning to trust *myself*."

With the first choice, you are shutting yourself down, compounding the original wound and hurting yourself. With the latter choice, you are opening up and growing, healing yourself.

Everything That Happens, Even Difficult and Terrible Things, Can Bring Unexpected Gifts To Receive Them, We Must be Willing to Unwrap Them

If you are willing to make your way through life's painful brambles, you will inevitably come upon juicy berries, too. This is not to say we rejoice in hardship, nor condone vile behaviors, but as we digest and assimilate what has happened or is happening, we will discover hidden gifts. One hint is this: these unasked for, golden gifts will almost always reveal and nourish the enormity of our capacity to love.

There Is Much Good Medicine in a Cup of Tea

The simplest things in life, like a kind word at just the right moment, are often the most deeply meaningful and transformative. In the same way, simple remedies often work best, even in the most complicated of situations.

Nothing Is a Distraction From Your Life, or Keeping You From Your Life; It Is *All* Your Life, Moment to Precious Moment

When we are dealing with bureaucracy and have to fill out excessive paperwork, or are in a traffic jam, it's easy to feel precious moments of our lives are being stolen! And yet, by putting frustration with what is, ahead of simply being present with what is, it is we who are stealing precious moments from our lives, not the paperwork, nor the traffic.

Mind and Body in the Same Place at the Same Time

When you find yourself tripping over random objects and bumping into the furniture, it's time to bring your mind and body back together. Rushing ahead mentally, or being stuck in thoughts of the past, can lead to minor accidents and more serious calamities. The body is a wonderful teacher of presence.

Try this: Stop. Stand still and repeat the invocation above. Say it **aloud** at least three times to reunite your mind and body. This simple practice can work wonders.

Stand Your Ground
Root in Integrity
Rise in Love

Claim your space, your right to exist.
Get to know who you truly are. Reach out to
share your unique expression
of love with others.

When Your Mind is Racing and You're Getting Nowhere Fast, Tune Into Your Body

Do this in whatever way works for you.

Dance. Walk in nature. Run. Practice yoga. Garden. Find what helps you drop out of your mind and sink into the sensations of your body—not to achieve a goal, but as its own experience.

Bodies Tell the Truth

We push and pull our bodies. We judge them and seek to shut them up when they are presenting unwelcome messages, such as, *I'm hurting. I'm not happy. I'm hungry for something.*

Learn to listen to your body, to feel, honor, and respect it. Your body is your constant companion throughout your life.

You Are a Human Being, or Better Still, a Human *Becoming*, Not a Human Doing

Breathe. Relax inside. Be kind to yourself.

Trees Remind Us That We Grow Down as Well as Up; Invisibly, as Well as Visibly

Growth is not always obvious; we grow inside ourselves, not just externally. Tree roots spread under the ground, mirrored by branches that grow up and out to the sky.

With time and practice, our inside and outside will come to reflect each other beautifully.

Whenever You Heal Some Hurt, Wounded Place Inside of You, It Helps Heal Something in Every One of Us

When we heal old wounds that once festered inside, it deepens our compassion for self and others. Compassion, by its nature, is expressed by being shared; our healing ripples out to our families, communities and the world.

What Is Good For The Earth Is Good For You, and For Us All

Our health and the health of the Earth are inextricably intertwined. Let this truth that is astoundingly complex, and yet so simple that children understand it perfectly, inform and guide our choices.

Let's treat ourselves and the earth "like dirt," meaning, with deep respect.

Joy Is Medicine

Cultivate joy.
Choose to do at least one thing today that brings you joy.

The Story You Tell Yourself and Others About What Has Happened, Determines What Happens Next

There is always another way to look at something. Is there a more healing way to re-frame your story?

Listen

Shhh … quiet your mind. Slow down and take a deep breath. Whether you're sitting at your desk or you're on the move, set aside time, regularly, to listen to your inner voice and to nature.

Guidance Is Available

Sometimes you need to ask within. Sometimes you need to ask another. Sometimes you need to ask the river. All require asking for help, and listening with an open, yet discerning mind to the guidance that will surely come.

Life Is Meant to Include the Bitter as Well as the Sweet

Just as bitter plants aid our physical digestion and emotional well-being, this flavor of experience is necessary to becoming a whole human being.

When we assimilate our bitter experiences, taking in any nourishment they offer, such as increasing our capacity for empathy, we grow.

As we learn to let go, and eliminate anything left behind that is not useful, such as resentment, we evolve.

Guilt Is Worthless Unless it Leads to Genuine Remorse; Remorse Is Invaluable

Guilt is child-like; it makes a sticky situation all about *you* and shuts down honest communication.

Remorse is a more mature response to feeling badly about something you've done or not done; it's concerned with resolutions, with finding a way to facilitate the well-being of another.

Remorse opens the door to taking responsibility, to making amends in the present and doing things differently in the future.

Sometimes You Have to Go Backward Before You Can Move Forward

When you're unable to move beyond something that went wrong because you believe it was "your fault," open a portal to the past and re-do the scenario in a meditation. Knowing what you know now, imagine yourself making another choice; envision and feel it fully, not as an act of denial, but as an act of creation.

This exercise invites emotional healing in the present and sets a new template for the future.

Make Space in Your Life

Whether you clear out a closet, drop something from your weekly schedule, or take time to meditate, creating space creates the kind of spaciousness that allows good things, people and opportunities a place to come in.

You Are Always on Your Path

It's impossible for you not to be. Wherever you are, your path is under your feet, at least metaphorically, whether you're climbing a mountain, rolling down the street in a wheelchair, flying to a far-off destination, or even hiding under the covers.

If you don't like where you keep finding yourself, turn and choose a different direction, or at least begin to imagine one. Regardless of what can feel like seemingly endless detours, you are always on your path home.

Everything Is Alive

There are no inanimate objects. The same breath of life, the same Divine Spirit, animates us all.

We Are Living and Dying in Every Moment

We are taught not to accept death, though this is a losing proposition that keeps us living more fearfully than fully. Even the cells in our bodies are continuously dying and being replaced with new ones. Partner consciously with the process of dying by releasing something, anything at all.

You could choose a fear, a resentment, or an unhealthy relationship. Or start with something tiny. Practice letting go. You'll become more fully alive.

Follow Your Original Instructions

Anishinaabe herbalist Keewaydinoquay said, "Of all creatures, the plants have remained truest to their original instructions. They give of themselves generously for the health of all beings."

Are you listening for your original instructions? If you've found them, are you following them? If not, please do. We need you and your gifts.

Almost Everything Worthwhile Takes Dedication and Patience

Learning a new language or how to play an instrument takes time and practice.

Healthy relationships, like gardens, can take years to become established. You don't need to be great or even good at something to dedicate yourself to it. Give yourself permission to enjoy the process.

Believing Is Something You Do
Knowledge Is Something You Gain
Wisdom Is Something You Have

You might feel pressure to defend a belief you hold dear. Like knowledge, belief implies something external, separate from you.

Wisdom, once earned, is inside you.
It can't be taken from you.

Own Your Gifts

We are told to "own our power" to change things in our lives and in the larger world. But we may meet this directive with ambivalence, because power is so frequently associated with domination and abuse. Try replacing the word "power" with the word *gifts*.

Own your gifts. Develop and use your gifts for the benefit of yourself and others.

You Are Not Too Old to

———————

Fill in the blank with whatever it is: take tango classes, go to college, paint murals.

Maybe, I admit, there are a few things it's unrealistic to set your sights on at a certain point; you probably won't become a prima ballerina if you start dancing at age 96, but don't let that hold you back from dancing!

Try: I'm old enough to know what I want, and now have the follow-through to pursue it!

PS: You can also make your own version of this: I am not too _____ to _____.

Whatever You Struggle With Externally, Also Mirrors a Place That Needs Peace and Healing Internally

Perhaps you struggle with how someone is treating you. Do you treat yourself well? Maybe you are an activist for social justice. Are you fair and just to yourself?

Strive to bring kindness to your inner struggles. True change begins within and ripples outward.

Love Heals

Love doesn't ask for anything. It simply is.
Invisible. Potent. Impossible to fully define. And
whether it is expressed gently or fiercely, love is
the most powerful healing force on Earth.

Flowers Encourage Bright Spirits

Wild flowers in a meadow, or cut flowers in a vase on your kitchen table, brighten the immediate atmosphere. When you eye lights on a flower, your spirit smiles.

The Best Way to Get Where You Want to Go Is to Practice Being Present Where You Are

The plants are our best teachers of this. Deep-rooted plants offer a clear mirror of rooting to rise, of growing into ourselves from a place of presence.

Allow Yourself to Daydream

It is restful and restorative to meander along the inner rivers and pathways of your thoughts, following the images and sensations that arise.

Not needing to achieve anything, nor to fill your inner spaces with other's stories and images may spark your creativity. Or you can just enjoy daydreaming.

Bodies Always Speak to Us in the Language of Love

Our bodies will even get sick to help us learn to love and accept ourselves. Please don't think the solution is to figure out what you "did wrong."

Look for ways you can bring more loving care to yourself and, by extension, to the Earth.

Know What Is Non-negotiable in Your Relationships

When you are clear on what is essential and what is unacceptable, you can be more flexible about everything else.

This nurtures harmony in our hearts and homes, and fosters more peace in the world.

Plants Are Our Elders, Teachers, and Allies

Sit with a plant and consciously inhale and exhale together for at least a few minutes.

You can simply be together with no agenda beyond connection, but if you humbly ask for a bit of wisdom from the plant and receive a message, it will be the perfect one for you in that moment.

Nothing Is More Magical and Mysterious than Reality

If you doubt this, witness a baby of any species being born, or hold the hand of a beloved as they die. The ongoing transformation of energy to matter and matter to energy reflects the magical, mysterious essence of reality.

This Is the Time of Everything There Are as Many Realities as There Are People

This is a time of unparalleled creative flux in how we view reality, and our viewpoints shape what we experience. The people you disagree with are looking through a different lens, and may believe they are seeing the one and only truth. It can be dizzying and divisive, but it's important to open dialogues with one another.

See if you can find even one point of agreement to begin a conversation. This brings more peace into our hearts and into the world.

Other Animals Have So Much to Teach Us

When you connect with animals deeply in life, or in meditation, or when you ingest their bodies with respect and gratitude as food and medicine, they become part of who you are.

If you choose to consciously embody their best attributes, you will become wiser and wilder than you were before.

Life and Death Are Not Opposites

Death feeds life.

When plants die and decompose, they give their nutrients back to the ground in which we grow our food. Compost kitchen scraps and watch them become fertile soil.

Make friends with the truth that life is fed by both birth and death; embrace life as it is.

Flexibility and Adaptability Nourish Your Resilience And Support Our Species' Evolution

Cultivating these qualities will help you sail more smoothly when turbulent waters rise up in your personal life, and they are essential as we engage in and move through the evolutionary chaos of the times we're living in with less fear and anxiety.

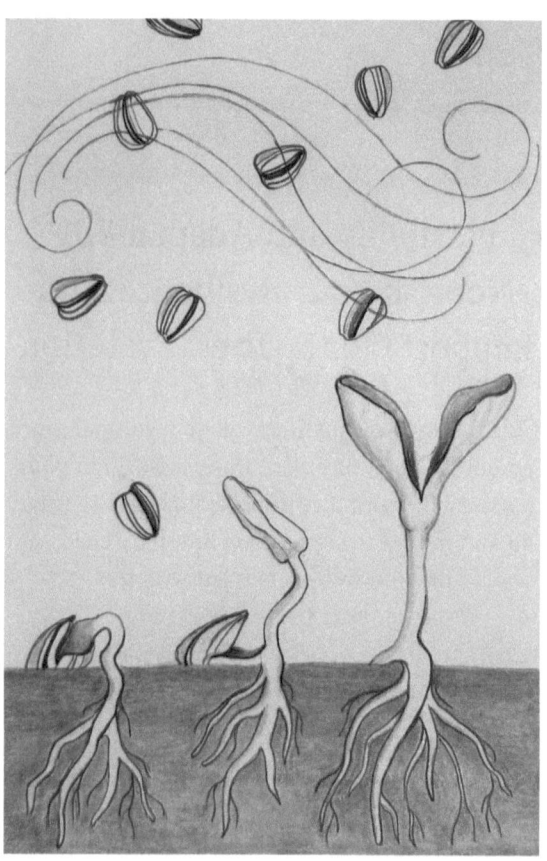

Imagine and Give Voice to the Best Possible Outcome

Be mindful of your thoughts. Take a step back and witness where your mind goes. Pay attention to your words. "I can't do that" can become, "I can't do that … yet!" When you are stuck in a loop of anxiety or fear about a particular potential future, make a conscious choice to imagine the best that could happen!

Imagination seeds physical reality.

Whatever Part of Yourself You Try to Get Rid of Will Stick to You like Glue

From the scaredy-cat to the raging fiend inside, we tend to project our unwelcome aspects onto others rather than risk meeting them in ourselves.

When parts of you that you see as negative are allowed to exist, they stop turning up at the worst possible moments just to get your attention.

Humor can help. When I catch myself sitting in judgment of someone, I imagine donning a white wig and wielding a gavel; this makes me laugh and fall off my high horse!

Your Purpose in Life Is to Become Yourself
What You Do, as Yourself, Will Follow Naturally

This is the prime directive, the first and foremost calling of a human life. As Shakespeare said, "To thine own self be true." Devote yourself to this and your life becomes richer and more meaningful, whatever your outward circumstances.

Breathe In
Ah, Life.
Breathe Out
Ah, Death.
Pause.
Repeat.

This simple practice of inhaling life and releasing it on your exhalations invites you to become friends with the inevitable passage we call death.

Begin to feel for what is eternal in you;
This sets you on your path of inner freedom.

We Are Made of Air, Fire, Water, Earth, and Spirit
The Elements Are Our Ancient Guardians,
And They Are Us, Writ Large

We live within a wheel of Air, Fire, Water, and Earth. The circle transforms into a spiral, held from below, watched over from above, and centered in the creative consciousness we call Love. We are always standing in the center of the wheel—the magical space where the individual self joins the oneness of all that is, each nourishing the other.

We are diverse expressions of indivisible unity.
One heart.
One love.

As We Come Home to Ourselves, We Inevitably Come Together to Create a Healthy World

When we are at peace inside ourselves, at home in our own skin, we transcend our sense of separation from others and realize we are one in infinite forms.

Everyone, human and more than human, matters deeply.

Acknowledgments

I've woven together this tapestry of teachings from many sources. It would be impossible for me to name all of my human and more than human teachers, so I'll simply say this:

My heart is overflowing with gratitude for all I've received, and for the opportunity to share what I continue to practice.

I'm grateful to Gail Stoughton for her evocative illustrations, Laney Britten for her graphic art magic, and Nicla DiCosmo for designing the perfect book cover.

These big little life tips are ones that have stood the test of time and all manner of circumstances. May you find helpful inspiration and good guidance here, as I have.

www.ingramcontent.com/pod-product-compliance
Lightning Source LLC
Chambersburg PA
CBHW031419290426
44110CB00011B/447